Dear Band Director:

Your Guide To Understanding the Color Guard

Shelba L. Waldron

ISBN: ISBN-10: 1539586723
ISBN-13: 978-1539586722

DEDICATION

To dedicate this book to one singular person would be wrong. Our activity is a great one that dates back generations. We are an art that has been built upon the threads of passion in the quest to put our stamp on the national arts scene. We have created a unique and undeniable niche that touches literally thousands of young people every year. This book is dedicated to every performer, designer, technician, judge, volunteer, board member, and parent that has poured their heart and soul into this, our art. Mostly though, I dedicate it to all the performers who came before me and paved the way for my moment on the field. With that being said, I must with all my heart thank David Baker....my first guard instructor. He was hard on me. He never gave up on me. He helped shape who I am today and remains a good friend thirty years later.

ACKNOWLEDGMENTS

This book would not have been possible without the support of my family who endured my many weekends teaching and judging color guard and then coming home to pour it out through words, while I sat at my computer with a glass of wine late into the night. I would like to also thank my mom who diligently played my tough, but very frank editor. Heather Rothman who kept telling me to write, write, and write some more. Brad Tilley who helped me market the book and get it to print. Tim Hinton at the Marching Roundtable for letting me participate in podcasts and creating an environment where all issues related to the pageantry arts can be discussed. To Jeff Bridges who took time out of his busy schedule to offer my first and honest critique. Finally, to Ron Comfort, Mike Marcantano, Bob Thomas and the entire Paradigm Winter Guard family who have always been there supporting me every step of the way.

Table of Contents

INTRODUCTION

“Do the difficult things while they are easy and do the great things while they are small. A journey of a thousand miles must begin with a single step.”—Lao Tzu

In the midst of directing a marching band, managing parent boosters, and day to day adolescent behaviors, a band director must also oversee the color guard with its staff, performers, and parents that come with it. It can be a daunting task, but with a little bit of goal setting, solid planning, and a vision of how the color guard will synergistically fit into the overall music ensemble, the journey of a thousand miles becomes a manageable and even enjoyable journey.

Color guard is a passion for many people who have grown up and lived in the world of the marching arts. It is a necessary component of a competitive marching band and, as small or large as it may be, the color guard comes with its own set of idiosyncrasies, hidden rules, and quirky artists. It is its own art form that consists of not just the use of standard color guard equipment such as flags and rifles, but has grown to incorporate sophisticated levels of dance, costuming, staging, theater, and even conditioning. When I began my career in color guard as a performer in 1986, dance as a driver of the equipment book was in its infancy. Floor tarps didn't exist. Winter Guard music was played on tape recorders and computerized edited soundtracks were still over two decades away.

Much has changed and the advancements have taken us from just a component of the band to an essential visual element that elevates the program from marching band to marching art. With the advancement of science and passage of time, we can now teach with a greater understanding of the mind of the performers. Technology allows us to communicate and teach differently than we did back in the 80's and 90's. Through the progressions of the science of body mechanics, we now know more about how to condition the body for what has become as much sport as it is art.

Even with all of these developments, the foundation of the activity is still the same. Training of the body, equipment, and mind remains a crucial factor in success. Choreography continues to evolve and the training that accompanies that choreography changes as well. Young people are joining the color guard in unprecedented numbers as color guard becomes more artistic, but the reason for participating hasn't changed since day one. Kids are looking for a place to make friends, fit in, and have a little fun in the process.

This book will explain why guard instructors do what they do and how to build the best program from the ground up for those with few resources to those who are resource rich. This is for the band director who inherited a color guard as an aspect of the marching band, but came to realize it was so much more than they bargained for under the job heading of "other duties as assigned." It is for the parent whose daughter came home one day with a flag pole and said she just joined the color guard and the parent said, "You joined the what?"

This book will attempt to break through the mystery of understanding the language guard people speak and the drama that is sometimes created. It is a look at the money needed for success, but when to say no to the spending of the money. It's a look at the staff members needed to create the guard most fitting for your band and your community, with a breakdown of who those people are and what their focus should be. Overseeing a color guard can be complicated, but it doesn't have to be if you take one step at a time and exert a lot of patience, sprinkled with the lessons we teach the kids themselves: communication, teamwork, and self-discipline.

This book is for anyone out there who wishes to understand at a deeper level the core concepts of color guard. Those at the top didn't just get there yesterday and most of them have failed and with that failure they have learned. So as I begin this book and as you turn the page to chapter one, you will learn that the lessons are not complicated, but simple and honest. They come from a place of passion and the betterment of our art. It is for you, the reader to ponder, debate; disagree with and contemplate, for dialog will only help us grow and make all of us a better student of the art we call color guard.

1 WELCOME TO YOUR BAND ROOM

Good morning and congratulations on your new job! You walk into your new band room and find that the office is yours. You scope out the practice rooms. You look at the inventory of instruments. Yes the program you are taking over has had some struggles. They don't have the money that the band down the street has. They have struggled and the school support for the band has never been strong. It doesn't matter. YOU are going to turn this ship around. This is now your band room. These are your instruments and it is your office. These are your musicians. You are excited.

You are trained, educated, and ready to go. You spy that perfect spot to hang your degree on the wall. You grab your degree in its wooden frame and place it on the wall to get a good visualization of how it will look as parents come into your office for meetings. You turn back around to place the degree back on your desk and there it is. Through the window of the office you spot it. It's tall, it's awkward, and a total mystery. When school ended it wasn't put away, almost as a tease to remind you that with your new job comes an inheritance of the color guard. Congratulations! You are now the official owner of the 6-foot flag pole staring across from you like an evil sorcerer with pinwheels for eyes. What in the hell you will do with those kids in your program who want to spin a flag over playing a flute begins to haunt you.

So what do you need to know? How can you build a program that is inclusive of the color guard and builds upon your music program as opposed to destroying it? How do you hire the right staff? How much money should be allocated for the guard? How much time should you, as the band director, spend with the color guard? How do you hire, fund, and include something that no one has trained you to understand?

Many reading this book will inherit a program that is already a fully functioning program. Your first job is to listen to those staff members, students, and parents who have been with the band for several years and take into consideration their concerns and honor their traditions. Those who are still around that helped build the program, are hoping you respect what they have built. Then there are the band directors who are the recipient of the brand new school, the one that has no history or traditions. Everything is fresh and pristine. There is no color guard and there is no band. All aspects of the music program must be built from the ground up. For purposes of this book, we are going to start with a program that is in need of new a guard staff. You know that the color guard needs to be a priority of the visual element of the music program, but funding allocation from the school is low, and you have seen other band programs where the color guard staff have rotated through much like a merry-go-round. You know that to succeed you must hire the right person and advocate for money with your parent booster organization. Recruitment of performers must become a priority if your desire is to have a competitive marching band. You realize that there isn't a lot of time to conduct an exhaustive search for the right person and get them through the bureaucratic processes required by your school system. You have to move fast, but you also must move with deliberate intent. To move with intent will require you, the band director, to look at your program with honest eyes.

Where is the program at right now?

What is the retention rate of the guard?

Is there a history of having large numbers of freshman, but few seniors?

Have you reviewed past rosters?

Have you looked at past videos of the band to get a grasp of what the color guard looked like in previous years?

What is your philosophy of marching band?

Do you want a competitive or a show band?

What type of booster organization do you have?

Is the booster organization supportive of a color guard or do they find them to be a nuisance?

These are the questions you must first ask yourself along with key staff, parents, and students of the program. So here we go. Let's start a color guard.

2 The Performers Who Join Color Guard

It has been known for quite some time that those who gravitate to the marching band are some of the brightest, most disciplined, and well behaved students in the school. Because of the vast amount of time spent together, these kids form lifelong bonds. Band members support each other and build each other up. All youth need to belong and as their brains and bodies develop, so does their need for healthy social environments where they form age appropriate bonds and work in a team setting. The color guard members are on a quest in school to find a niche' they can call home.

Color guard is the visual element of the band, seen with equipment and props, that helps bring the show to life. It involves dance and sometimes elements of theater. Sometimes when young people join the color guard, it is simply out of curiosity, "Well let me check this out and see what it's all about."

Color guard is not a household name in the extracurricular community. When a boy comes home and tell his parents that he is trying out for the baseball team, it's easy for them to understand what it is involved. They might even already know what the financial responsibilities and time commitments will be. This holds true for most all traditional activities in school such as cheerleading, football, volleyball, soccer, and any other mainstream sport you might see on E.S.P.N. Even marching band is easy for most people to understand as you see marching bands in parades and at football games. Color guard is different, as it is a specific section within the marching band that is rarely considered as its own separate entity by a neophyte to the marching arts. Don't even think about explaining winter guard to the parent who has yet to grasp the color guard as a part of the marching band.

Color guard members find their way to the color guard through many means. Some are invited by friends and others are former musicians who want to explore a different avenue of the marching activity. Some join the color guard because it offers a form of dance, performance, and creativity that isn't available to them through traditional means. Many are girls who don't fit the traditional female archetype, thus leaving them out of activities such as cheerleading and the dance team. Many of the performers found that they didn't have the skills to follow the traditional route of sports.

The majority of all color guard performers in America are female. This is important. The color guard, if large enough, could be the principal female based activity within the high school. It can be an awesome entity within your band program that gives girls a place to call their own. Additionally, color guard will often attract males. Some of those males will be gay. That isn't meant to generalize boys who join color guard, but the fact is that many male guard members are gay and the guard could very well be the only place they feel comfortable.

There isn't a perfect way of defining the type of person that ends up in color guard. The color guard activity is first and foremost a youth based sport that attracts thousands of young people every year and most of those young people are teenage girls. Having a base understanding of the issues and challenges young women face goes a long way in retaining the performers year after year. For example, body image greatly impacts the self-esteem of teen girls, primarily because they grow up in a nation where the idea of beauty is a multi-billion dollar industry set up to make women feel bad about themselves. Having the perfect weight is a cornerstone in the industry of beauty and although we are making great strides in bringing awareness to the fact that inner beauty is more important than outer beauty, there is still a long way to go in changing the 360 degree media culture our young people are surrounded by. This media culture tells children every day that they aren't "enough." Understanding this concept helps in how you speak to, educate, and even costume young women.

Maybe it's best to just say that guard members are just regular every day kids who merely want to belong to something special. That's the key. The guard is special and no matter how they find their way to the marching band, it's important that the band director, staff, and booster organization treat the color guard with the respect they deserve and as an equal participant within the music program.

So, when a student joins the guard, it is often a mystery to both them and their parents. There simply aren't mainstream models in real world media for someone who doesn't understand color guard to find a guide. For a potential performer to survive in the color guard, they have to learn to embrace the feeling of awkwardness that comes with holding a flag for the first time. Then they have to be taught to march and spin that flag at the same time. Many will dance for the very first time in their life and as they do that, they must become able to do it in time with the person next to them. Some of them barely understand concepts of rhythm and tempo. These concepts are all new to them and it is overwhelming. For every new skill they learn, they must then be comfortable performing in front of a crowd and in a costume that may or may not fit in their comfort zone.

As time goes by, the new guard member becomes the seasoned guard member who feels confident in their own color guard skin. They welcome new challenges to help build their own personal repertoire. Some will take leadership roles within the band program and some will move on to college marching band, drum corps, or an independent winter guard. That scared 8th grader who, "*just wanted to see what it is all about*" has been bitten by the pageantry bug and becomes the next generation of instructors, designers, and technicians. Those instructors are passionate and will work late into the night listening to music, writing choreography, designing costumes, and responding to parent emails.

No matter how someone comes to the color guard activity, what makes them stay is how we as instructors' coach them and educate them.

3 Finding the Right Guard Director

So this is where we begin. It easy to put out the word to your friends and post on Facebook that you are looking for a guard director, but knowing what you are hiring for is a complex concept and is not as easy as taking the first flag spinner that replies to your Facebook request. The art of color guard has evolved over the years in such a way that there are actual debates as to whether color guard is more sport than art or more dance than equipment. You are going to need someone who will understand these concepts, but knows how to use the sport, the art, dance and equipment at the appropriate levels and at the appropriate times. You will need someone who has the ability to take a hard look at where the activity is currently, but also where the performers and program are and where it fits both locally and nationally within the current artistic and training structures of color guard.

What is this activity all about anyway? You were in

marching band. Maybe you were in drum corps. You've possibly watched winter guard videos...you think you know what color guard is. You think. It's easy to watch a video and say, "That's what I want. Who teaches that color guard?" To build the competitive marching band program that is expected of you, you must understand that just like the time and commitment it takes the marching band to achieve greatness, is the same amount of time it takes to build a great color guard. It can't be rushed and you must have patience with the process. You must also understand that, color guard is an industry. There is a lot of money to be made on the backs of the parents that support your program and if you don't hire carefully, the wrong instructor will suck the parents financially dry, forcing a pattern of low retention, thus creating low levels of recruitment. With just the click of the mouse a person can buy their design, drill, choreography, costumes, silks, and everything in between. Everything in the activity can be bought and many instructors think that the more you buy the better you'll be. Take caution with that philosophy, however, and of the person who doesn't know the value of the budget and how the money is raised. If you do not hire a guard director that understands the business of the industry and the art of coaching young people, you will never see the greatness your marching band could become. You ultimately want to find a team player: someone who works well with the kids, parents, school administration, and other staff members. Your guard director and the staff they hire represents the band program when you aren't around. Hire carefully.

The color guard is the primary visual element of your band. They are the ones out in front at pep rallies, football games, and parades by the sheer nature of the large flag pole they carry and the costume they wear that separates them from the band. How they look, how they stand, and the pride they take in their role with your band can make or break how the community sees the guard and fundraises for it. Yes, they are an equal part of the band, but they are the beauty element within the pageantry that the community comes to know. Your guard director must understand these concepts.

Often times when guard instructors are hired, the interview questions focus on the pageantry element of where someone has marched and concepts of design. Money is often a distant third within the process of interviewing prospective directors and instructors.

Where have you marched?

Who have you designed for?

Can you choreograph?

Do you have a video I can watch of your previous guard?

Then comes the uncomfortable money question and many if not most of the people in color guard hate the money conversation.

How much do you charge?

Or

I can only offer you "x" amount of dollars a month. I know that isn't a lot, but we could always try to work something out or if you can't help us, could you just come in a few times until we find someone we can afford?

Money is fluid and your ability to negotiate is easier for some programs than others, but poor decisions have been made regarding the hiring of staff based on the uncomfortable money conversation when either one or both parties aren't up front with what they have or what they need. Band directors who feel they need to spend money they don't have or their inability to negotiate will ultimately put their program at financial risk. Before you even put the word out that you are in need of a color guard director, the first thing you should know is how much you have to spend and who you are looking for.

Do you want someone young that will grow with the program or do you want a nationally minded person that will fast track the program? These are important questions that relate directly to the means and goals of the program.

Hiring Consideration:

When interviewing a person to take over the color guard, inquire about longevity at previous programs.

The interview questions referenced above are all valid questions, but they don't get to the heart of who you are hiring and oftentimes they stop there. Many instructors come from programs where several staff members were responsible for the success of the band or guard, so be sure to ask your prospective director what their specific role was and ask for references.

So what questions should you ask during the interview process? Always use open ended questions. Require the applicant to speak to a knowledge of the industry, ***coaching with deliberate intent*,** financial management, parental engagement, philosophy of recruitment, team building, and team involvement. If you notice, none of these concepts have even begun to touch on whether the person can design a show or clean a phrase, but you have to ask yourself again, "Who am I hiring and how long do I want this person to stay here?"

***Coaching with deliberate intent is the concept that a person who works with young people approaches rehearsal methodically; keeping in mind the unique attributes of the youth they are working with**.*

"But, I don't have a lot of money to pay for a good person and I don't have a lot of time. No one would take what I can afford if they had to go through an intensive interview process."

That's a valid statement and a legitimate concern and I counter with this question.

Are you hiring for seasonal survival or hiring to build? One will take you down a revolving and repetitive path and the other will give you peace of mind. One path is easy and one is not. One of those paths could cost you your job and the other path could turn your band into a competitive name.

Color guard is an industry, a multimillion-dollar industry to be exact, and money is important. However, your band isn't the first one to have a small budget and it won't be the last. Sometimes the smallest budget, can create the mightiest giant, in our world of pageantry. It's how you hire in the beginning and your willingness to be patient throughout that process is what makes the difference.

"But band camp is right around the corner and I need someone that can choreograph the guard work."

This is also a valid concern. What if the guard director you are looking to hire isn't a very good choreographer? What if they aren't a great designer? Here's the easy answer to that question. The director you want will be able to design for the band you are hiring them for, as they will understand that they first must build the skills of the performers before they can write choreography for young people that have yet to be trained. The choreographer you need for the band you are planning is not the one you need at this stage. Effective choreography is just a byproduct of great training and right now you don't have either. Your director will understand that thoughtful design does not need complicated choreography. A director that communicates well with the design staff, staging and drill that is inclusive of the color guard, and well planned visual effects will produce a better product than a color guard that is separated as an afterthought to the production and complicated choreography. If the guard is taught to stand up straight...spin together...and look into the eyes of the audience, they will have already beaten half the color guards out there. The right director will know that the color guard is not a separate entity of its own, but a crucial aspect of the general effect, individual analysis, and ensemble analysis. Sometimes the best design is one that demonstrates great training and pride over choreography and confusion.

Terminology Update:

Choreography is the written material placed on top of the staging. It is sometimes referred to as the written book or the vocabulary.

So who is it you are hiring for this color guard that is possibly new or struggling to maintain a consistent staff? The person you are looking for is a **manager.** You are looking for someone who can manage the day-to-day details, but who can also articulate a realistic vision encompassing short and long terms goals. Yes, the person does need to know the basic fundamentals behind equipment principles, movement, conditioning, and design.

They must first, however, be a manager who understands the "how" of running the color guard and not just the "what" in terms of writing a show. Most of the people who apply or who you find will be young. Some are in college and have just aged out of drum corps or winter guard. Some have started careers and others teach color guard part time and work in a part-time industry such as bartending or retail. Regardless of who they are, most will be young and will need your support.

By applying the following questions, you can start to understand who is the best fit for your program.

What is your philosophy on recruitment of new kids?

How comfortable are you at interacting with parents and boosters?

Can you give me an example of a time when you worked with a parent to resolve an issue with their child?

Give me some examples of how you plan to set the program up for financial success.

What does leadership mean to you?

Can you give me some examples of how you continue developing your skills and knowledge of the activity?

Do you have a mentor you consult with on a regular basis?

How often do you expose yourself to new concepts related to youth development, art, or dance?

Can you give me an example of how you have worked in the past with drill writers, designers, and other members of the band staff?

Give me an example of how you have worked to resolve differences in opinions related to the design of the show.

What is your knowledge base of the current judging criteria for color guard in this region?

The list of questions can go on and on. The key is to create questions that generate dialog and discovery. Most importantly, don't forget to ask for and check **references.** The right candidate will speak less of medals and more of the process of achievement of that medal. They will talk about the team they worked with and how the team was important to success, because no good program achieved success based on just one person. Remember, you are hiring someone who can build the program with you or destroy it in the blink of an eye. This is your job and your career. This is not the time to throw caution to the wind and hire the first person that answers your ad.

A well run interview is not just for you to decide whether or not the candidate is a good fit for your program, but for the candidate to decide if your band is also a good fit for them. It is an opportunity for dialog and discovery. Since many of the potential instructors are young or inexperienced, it is an opportunity to identify strengths and weaknesses so it will be easier for you to know where to offer assistance and possibly hire additional staff, if needed. In some regions of the country instructional staff may be limited, so although the candidate may not be the perfect fit, the interview will help you know where your limitations will be.

"But I need someone for band camp. I need someone to stand in front of the kids. Right Now!"

Yes, you do. But keep in mind that while you just need someone to stand in front of the kids, the kids are looking for someone to lead them. I guess that's your catch-22. What happens when the clock is running out and you can't find a person who wants to take on your program as a director? Maybe there isn't anyone in the area who can fill the need, or you can't find a full time person capable of taking on the program for reasons that relate to time or money. This is common and yes, it is a problem.

You do this. You put the word out through every social media platform you can find and every message board in the country and advertise that you are looking for a person with a strong understanding of teaching the technical aspects of color guard. You are looking for someone who can teach basic equipment fundamentals, movement technique, and posture. You need someone who wants to work with motivated kids and kids hungry for information. You are looking for someone for the season, but will take a month, a week, a day, or even an hour to have someone strong stand in front of the color guard and tell them that they matter and on that...you will find someone who just might step up to the plate. Some of the best programs have started with just that person. Be sure to reach out to your local winter guard and marching band circuits and, if you can, seek out the nearest independent winter guard as they may have performers who are looking for a program to work with. You just have to have patience.

Example Ad:

"Wanted. Guard instructor to work with up and coming band program. Are you looking to work with a band that has a supportive band director?

Motivated boosters? Hard working kids who are looking for someone to lead them to greatness? If so, we are the band for you."

Cheesy? Absolutely. However, the ad speaks to the three things guard instructors struggle with the most: band directors who aren't supportive, boosters who aren't motivated, and kids who don't want to work.

Additionally, don't forget the genius technology has brought the activity. Applications such as Skype and Facetime are allowing consultants to attend rehearsal and offer real time feedback. The quick access to video by phone allows another way to get a direct response to issues you may be having. Using techniques of consultation through video can help you identify problems with drill, flow of the equipment work, musicality, transitions, and training. It's an invaluable tool that is so often not utilized. If you find that after an exhaustive search for full time staff and you still can't find anyone, at the very least, utilize the benefit of technology.

If you hire someone to "just" stand in front of the kids, you will find that the staff you hire will not be invested in the program and you will rotate staff annually. This will demonstrate to the performers that the guard doesn't share the same value as the musicians and eventually those kids will look elsewhere to fill their free time. They will tell their friends that the guard is a waste of energy and money. They will complain to their parents. They will talk to their teachers. Remember, you are hiring a manager and that takes a significant amount of effort and there is no way of getting around it. You can count on luck or you can depend on diligence. Continue to look for the right person, while working closely with a temporary person that you trust.

Note: References must be checked. You are hiring someone to work with minors and this detail cannot be overlooked.

4 Staff Roles and Responsibilities

When putting together a color guard staff, it is important to understand the staff terminology commonly used in the activity. Your budget, will depend on how many of these individual people you should be hiring. Many of the roles described in this chapter can be taken on by one person, but it's rare that one person encompasses all the skills necessary, and even if they do, having additional people to offer feedback can be very helpful in identifying flaws in production of the show and in the processes of running the program. Sometimes these people can be considered consultants, such as a drill writer or choreographer, and others are considered a part of overall marching band staff.

The Design Team

Director:

- The manager of the team

- Takes the lead on administrative tasks such as budget creation, parental communication, and line item purchasing power
- Initial hiring/firing of additional staff
- Works with the design team to coordinate production value items needed such as costumes, silks, props, and floor tarps

The director sets the tone for rehearsals, scheduling, and time management. The director takes on many roles depending on the program. Sometimes they are the designer and sometimes they are the technician. Sometimes they are both.

Program Coordinator:

- During marching band season, this person will engage at the highest level with the design team
- Works with the caption heads/section leaders to coordinate the focus of rehearsal, changes to the show, and anything related to the overall production

Program coordinators are often considered part time staff that split their time with other programs. They are an additional staff cost, but many bands find program coordinators to be an asset that takes some programmatic duties off the shoulders of the band director.

Designer:

- Conceptualizes the show
- Oftentimes writes the drill or elements of staging
- Works with the caption heads on the coordination of the production to include music, drill, characterization, and production value.

Drill Writer:

- Writes the actual drill for the marching band or winter guard
- Often hired separately from the day to day staff
- Works from a distance, but for additional payments will often come to practices to help fix or restage the drill

Drill writers usually work under contract and have very specific line items as to what they are willing to do and not do. Be sure to read the contract carefully and communicate often with your drill writer.

Choreographers

Equipment

- The person who works with the designer to bring the production to life through the equipment phrasing

Movement

- The person who works with the designer to bring the production to life through the dance elements of the show

Technicians

Flag Technician

- This person's primary expertise lies within the cleaning of the flag line or flag book. They are often the person to creates the basic fundamentals for the flag line.

Weapon Technician

- This person's primary expertise lies within the cleaning of the rifle or sabre book.
- Create and teach the basic fundamentals for the weapons
- This position could easily be split between two roles as sabre and rifle are two

completely different pieces of equipment that are weighted and spun differently.

Movement Technician

- This person's primary expertise lies with the cleaning of the dance program.
- Responsible for designing a technical movement program such as how the guard will stretch, move through space, and basic ballet, jazz, and modern dance exercises

Drill/Foot Technician

- This person cleans drill and often is responsible for cleaning the band and color guard from the field based on the individual movement of the performers.

Personal Trainer/Conditioning Coach

- This person builds the exercise and conditioning program in tandem with the staff. They help the performers understand how their bodies can best be conditioned to manage the show with minimal impact.

This role is fairly new to the activity, but as the equipment and movement choreography evolves, this person is becoming more crucial.

It is important to recognize that these roles are separated out for the purposes of description and only those programs with the perfect financial scenario can have all of these positions filled with different people. Most band programs will need to review their budget and perform an analysis of the existing staff structure to figure out who on their staff can serve in multiple roles and which roles are expendable. It is important to not underestimate any of the staff members as a color guard equipment technician may also be able to serve as an overall foot technician for the band or a choreographer may be able to serve as a program coordinator. The key is to communicate clearly with the staff, understand where their strengths are and analyze where the programmatic weaknesses lie.

The question that you have to ask yourself is this.

What do I need the most to help build my program right now? What is more important to this program today?

I can't answer that question for any one person, but a starter program or program in disarray most likely needs a good director first. Hiring a person because of how they choreograph can lead to disaster if that person doesn't have the skills to manage money, personnel, time, and understand the processes of cleaning a phrase. You need to hire a manager and a leader, as a good leader will be able to analyze the strengths and weaknesses within the program and themselves, thus building the program methodically and with patience. Keep in mind that most programs, regardless of size, usually need at least two people to help it run fluidly. Two people working cohesively help ideas from becoming one sided. They keep each other in check and allows duties to be split so one can focus on training and cleaning, while the other focuses on design and choreography. Two people also help avoid burnout of your staff and allows the performers to receive information from different perspectives. Try budgeting for more than one guard person if the program has the capability to do so.

When hiring consultants to work with your program, be very clear with your intentions as to the work you want them to do. Don't waste their time and encourage your staff to listen and learn from them.

5 SETTING GOALS

Setting goals for the band and color guard program is actually fairly easy, yet is an overlooked task many instructors and band directors miss and this mistake is made over and over again. Setting goals is crucial in understanding how to budget for the show, hire staff, and fundraise. Setting goals fall into several categories, but if the goals are not discussed and set, then there is virtually no direction. In the most honest way to say it, many guard programs barely survive season to season because they lack organizational direction. When many color guards do set goals they tend to be more competitive in nature and don't take into account the steps it takes to achieve lofty goals. The color guard director should set goals with the band director, boosters, and students and not for them. For every color guard out there who has a forward thinking instructional staff, there are dozens more that have no idea where they are headed or how they plan to get there. Additionally, they have band directors who aren't engaged and leave the staff to their own devices.

First things first. As a band director with the overarching responsibility of the color guard, it is important to know that the guard will not reach any type of national status on a whim just because your staff believes they can design a great show. If they believe that then they have fooled themselves and you. It isn't realistic, and it will burn the program out well before glory can ever be achieved. Goals must be set for the short and long term. This is called strategic planning and can be and should be a yearly process with all major program stakeholders brought to the table:

- Staff
- Parents
- School Administration
- Community Partners
- Performers

**If the primary stakeholders are left out of the process of setting goals, then they will not be there to support you when needed.*

The first thing you should do after hiring your staff is to set realistic goals.

So what goals should you be setting with your

staff? There are 5 sets of goals to be addressed before planning of the design begins:

- Short term
- Long term
- Competitive
- Financial
- Recruitment

Once those goals are set, it is equally important to set into motion a solid plan on reaching said goals.

Short Term Goals

Where do you want to be at the end of the school year? What about the end of the current fall season? Where do you want to be at the end of band camp or the end of one singular rehearsal? These are short term goals and without them there is no way to gauge where you have been or where you are headed. Many instructors set goals that seem great when spoken out loud, but don't often take into account the work and money that go into achieving that goal.

"We are bringing out a winter guard this year and in two years we want to go to nationals."

O.K. great. That's a very admirable goal, but what

does that mean? Is it even achievable? Is it realistic? Can it be achieved under the current financial and rehearsal structure? How do the performers spin **today?**

"I want the guard to win their class by next season at state championships."

Ummm...sure. Gotcha. How is that going to occur? Do you know who your competitors are? Has the guard ever won anything in their history?

"I think we should do a show about war and we will dress the guard in 1940's costumes and they will play the role of the girl that was left behind."

No. Just no. This is not a goal. It is a show idea and it is one of the most common mistakes a band or guard program can make. Designing a show can only happen once the goals are laid out. If the staff lacks a general understanding of the performers and resources available, then problems will most certainly occur.

So what do short term goals look like? The famous acronym of S.M.A.R.T. is a good start.

Specific, Measurable, Agreed Upon Action, Realistic, and Time Bound

Do the goals have to be all encompassing? No,

but being "smart" about setting goals is a good place to start. While setting the goal through the SMART method is important, it is also just as important to follow that goal with an action.

Below is an example of a good short term goal. **Think of a short term goal as a flashlight that guides you down a dark path.**

"By the end of the season, we will have raised $3,000 through fundraising activities to be utilized in the future as a fund for students who cannot afford to participate in the winter guard."

S—To raise money for students who cannot afford winter guard

M—$3,000

A—Fundraising activities

R—(Realistic for your program and your community)

T—The end of the season

The "end of the season" is the timeframe. Raising "$3,000" is specific and it is measurable. The specific purpose is for "students who cannot afford winter guard" and the action is "through fundraising activities." The realistic aspect is with a discussion with those doing the fundraising, which is your booster organization.

Here is another good short term goal.

"By the end of the school year we will have recruited at least eight new incoming freshmen performers, who show an interest in participating in the upcoming marching band season."

This example gets to the heart of to whom you want to market the program and gives a number to reach. It implies where you must start the process to reach your goal. To get eight new freshmen performers to show interest, recruitment at the middle school is necessary. This indicates a concept of building toward the future. Setting a number allows you to measure your recruiting success over the course of several years and adjust the target accordingly.

There are multiple ways to set short term goals. They can be production goals set for a particular show or technical goals based on skill.

"By the end of September all members of all sections of the band will be able to demonstrate a solid understanding of the individual marching technique."

Short term goals should be set for one year or less and work in conjunction with the long term goals.

Long Term Goals

Long term goals are no different than a short term goal, except long term goals are usually a result of the work accomplished through the short term goal. They help guide the direction of the program for the next 3-5 years. If the short term goal is a flashlight, then the long term goal is the compass on a long path filled with roadblocks and obstacles trying to stop you and turn you back from where you came. The long term goal helps you move over those obstacles by constantly looking at and re-evaluating the actions to achieve the short term goals.

"Within three years, the winter guard will be trained well enough to successfully achieve the Box 5 criteria at the Regional A level."

This goal allows the entire staff to know where they are headed. It stops the process of rushing through the necessary steps for long term success and allows a monitoring of the program each year as you head toward that three-year mark. This particular goal allows the staff to design appropriately and have in depth discussions with judges and consultants on how to best guide them.

"By the end of year three, 70% of all parents will attend booster meetings and competitions to support their children.

Another example of a goal that is measurable and time bound and clearly speaks to who they are targeting and what they are attempting to accomplish.

One final note about creating short and long term goals. When setting these goals, all stakeholders need input, and research needs to be conducted to make the goals achievable. Many guard instructors will set a goal to be nationally or regionally competitive, but the reality is that those competitive color guards require a supportive booster organization that is willing to raise funds necessary for such a goal, and require performers who are willing to put the time in. Goals cannot be set in isolation of the stakeholders.

Competitive Goals

Simply put. Where do you want the color guard to be when the season is over? What is the realistic goal of competition for the size of the band/guard, financial capacity, parental support, ability of the performers, and ability of the staff? What is the realistic competitive goal for your area of the country? Some local areas have stronger high school programs than others and more support in terms of educational opportunities with knowledgeable practitioners of the pageantry arts. All of this must be taken into account when setting realistic competitive goals for any one season.

When setting goals for competitive success, the concept of success must also be defined and discussed. Programs that don't have a history of competitive success may simply define success as the ability of the performers to finish the season with a higher level of confidence and training than the year before. Competitive success could be defined by an increase of overall score than the previous year at various points in the season. To just define success by placement is not realistic as no one can control their competitors or the subjective art of judging.

Competitive goals should be set by demonstrating a thorough knowledge of the criteria the marching band show is judged against for not just the color guard, but all visual captions within the marching band as well. It is very possible that a new instructor with a new color guard can show competitive success within the color guard caption alone, but when the captions of General Effect or

Ensemble Analysis are factored in, then the color guard may or may not be helping the overall product if it is not well coordinated with the band as a whole.

"The color guard will place in the top three of their class at all marching band competitions by year three."

"The winter guard will be promoted from the Regional A class to the A Class within three years of starting the winter guard."

"The marching band will score at least an 80.0 in all visual captions by the end of the season."

Regardless of how you set your competitive goals, there should be a reality to them that remains consistent with the local competitive culture and criteria, as well as through an analysis of the history of the program.

Financial Goals

This is an important one. Setting a budget is crucial in the planning of a marching band program, but cannot be realistic without short term and long term planning. The hard part to setting a budget is figuring out how much you will need in order to reach your competitive aspirations. If you have followed the order of goal setting up to this point, then you will now need to set the financial goals of the program.

Financial goals have more to do with what the money is for than it does with how you plan on raising those funds. The financial goals are the guide to your fundraising. "How much" is what the budget is for. Your ability to raise those funds is the action taken after the goal is set. **Warning, this is the one goal that, if not taken seriously, will take the program down a path that you might not be able to return from before the school administration decides it is time to hire a more financially savvy band director**. Financial goals should be made in tandem with the short and long term goals of the program and most certainly with the parents that are paying the dues and planning the fundraisers. The business of the pageantry arts should never be taken lightly. When creating financial goals for a guard program, it is important to include all entities related to the band program as a whole, while looking at the individual ensembles for which the band program must fundraise, such as:

- Marching band
- Winter guard
- Concert band
- Percussion ensemble
- Spring trip

"By the end of year one, the music boosters will have raised 15% over the previous year to help offset costs for the winter guard program."

"Student fees for the marching band season will not go above $650 for the next two years."

"By the end of year three, the 501c3 that supports all ensembles of the music program will have acquired one major financial sponsor per separate ensemble."

"Each year a separate fundraiser will be planned to cover future capital expenses."

Financial goals, just like any other goal, are not written into stone and should be reviewed for progress and attainment on a frequent basis. These goals should be the basis for discussion at booster and staff meetings. Setting specific financial goals also sets a base expectation of all incoming families and staff members as to the direction of the program. Setting financial goals helps the community and school administration understand where you are headed and how they can help.

Recruitment Goals

The final major category of goal setting lies within the actual recruitment of staff members, performers, and their parents. When thinking about recruitment, you should be thinking about how the previous four goals have been written and what will be needed to achieve those goals. Programs should strive to make gains in either the addition of new performers for long term stability or the sustainability of the current performers. There is natural attrition as seniors leave, but goals should be set to replace those seniors and not to lose them before graduation.

"There will be a 15% increase in incoming freshmen for the following year."

"The attrition rate of the students will stay below 5% at the end of each school year."

As the program gets better and over time, it will be important to consistently evaluate your staff for needed areas of expertise. A goal for the staff may look like this.

"A program coordinator will be hired by year three to navigate the band program through the phases of preparing for regional level competition."

Setting goals are as individualized as they are multifaceted. No band or color guard should have goals that match the goals of any other program, as no program has the same problems or the same student body. It is simply irresponsible to hire a guard staff and let them to start buying items, recruiting kids, and talking with parents without a direction for where they are headed. This goes back to hiring your director. You are hiring for a business and the business is the pageantry arts, with youth as the consumer. You need someone who thinks strategically and can communicate the strategy to all involved.

Fundraising Tip:
Visual images help students, parents, and administration understand how far the program has to go when trying to reach a specific goal. Place the image just outside the door of the band room so everyone can see it when they walk by.

6 Budgeting for the Staff

"But I don't have a large budget," is the statement of the century spoken in just about every band room and on every campus in America. Let's go ahead and dispel the myths right now about the bands that have money or appear to have money. Bands that perform at the national level, who frequently travel, or appear to have a large staff with a large budget did not get there overnight and if they did, they are rare and hard to find. It takes years to create the competitive programs you see on the field at Bands of America or the floor at Winter Guard International. To create those programs takes patience and careful planning. It takes a staff that works well together and communicates their needs and concerns openly and freely to each other, the performers, and most importantly...the parents who are responsible for raising the funds.

Many band programs lack proper funds to buy instruments, much less guard equipment. Most color guards are poorly funded and many are an afterthought to the school administration. Many are functioning in Title One schools, where the parents don't have the spending power to pay the dues of their kids or offer transportation to and from practice. Travelling out of the county or state is difficult.

It is important to note, that according to a 2015 PEW Research Study, approximately eight in ten families who make above $75,000 a year report that their children participate in extra-curricular activities. As the income goes down and as expected, so does participation in activities. Families who make less than $30,000 annually, report that their children participate in extra-curricular activities at a rate of six in ten and the majority of those in that subgroup don't participate in teams that require travel. The lower the income and the lower base of the overall community income, the harder it will be to become a nationally based program without undue stress on the parents. This however does not mean that you still can't have a strong competitive marching band and color guard, as long as the budget and the design of the program is tailored to the resources of your community. All youth deserve the arts and as an activity of the arts, it is up to us as practitioners to find the means through sound budgeting and the creative use of resources.

So when you hire a guard staff, hire with a sense of caution and deliberate intent by analyzing the budget of the entire program and taking into account the means of the performers. Look at your staff budget in its entirety and make decisions on how you want to position the color guard within the structure of your program. If you decide that you have to pay a music arranger, drill writer, percussion staff, marching staff, and color guard staff, then make sure one entity of the staff is not sucking the money from the budget faster than the other. You can hire the best drill writer in the business, but if you don't have the color guard staff to bring that drill to life, then most likely the money will be wasted. If you've spent 50% of your staff budget on the percussion caption head, while leaving none for a marching technician, then all you really have is an above average percussion line with a below average marching band to back them up. Learn to negotiate with your designers and caption heads and then come to conclusions as to whether or not you really need them in this current season, or if you can hire them a couple of years down the road, after the building stage is complete.

So let's look at your budget. How much should you be paying your guard staff per line item and what should you expect them to do for the money?

Let's pretend that you have $4,500 to spend for the color guard staff during marching band season. This number does not include anything related to winter guard. Breaking the budget into line items will help the director you hire figure out how much to ask for personally and how much will be left to hire additional staff.

Scenario One

Director Salary--$2,000

Technician--$500

Part Time Choreographer-$1,000

Band Camp--$1,000

=$4,500

The director accepts $2,000 for themselves for the season, which includes attendance at all rehearsals, shows and works with the drill writer. They might then hire an inexperienced technician for $500 who can help run sets from the field. The band camp fee would be split between the two for $500 apiece, while hiring an additional choreographer to help write major effect moments for the remaining $1,000.

Scenario Two

Director Salary--$500

Technician(x2)--$1,000 per

Directors Writing Fee--$1,000

Band Camp--$1,000

=$4,500

In this scenario the director realizes they can't be at all rehearsals and competitions due to personal commitments to work, so they hire two strong technicians at one thousand each and then the director takes $500 for teaching and $1,000 for writing the show. You have $1000 left over for band camp that is split with the staff.

There are multiple scenarios. Some band programs do not include band camp in the overall guard budget, but as a specific line item for the overall music program. Other programs contract staff by the hour, while others give an overall seasonal fee to include design, training, attendance at shows, and face time with the performers. It's important to note that regardless of how you split the fees for the staff, all parties are on the same page and contracts are in place before the season begins.

Knowing what to pay is a difficult topic. We don't have a standard base as an activity, nor do we have hard data on salary based on expertise and results. So let's go back to the director you are about to hire and ask them a few questions.

"What is your background in the marching arts?"

(Are they at the beginning of their teaching career or do they have several success stories under their belt?)

"How much experience do you have directing programs?"

"What are your strengths and weaknesses?"

(Do they even have an awareness of their weaknesses?)

"Can you choreograph or will you have to hire someone to do that?"

"Do you have any documented expertise or certifications in areas such as dance, teaching, coaching, judging, theater, or other artistic avenues?"

"How much time do you expect to put into the program both in front of the performers and behind the scenes?"

Do you have a working knowledge of the judging criteria that the band and guard band will be judged against?"

"Would you consider yourself resourceful when purchasing equipment and costumes?"

If you find that the person answers the questions in such a way that demonstrates experience in directing, a working knowledge of the activity, and brings to the table an expertise in dance, judging or conditioning…then keep them and fight for them. Don't be afraid to negotiate. Often times you will find that most people aren't looking to make a living off of your program, they are just simply wanting to stay in the activity; to have a creative outlet and give back to the kids. These are important people. With experience comes wisdom. With a desire to further their education whether it be in college or through certifications, means they are willing to better themselves. While it is tempting to hire the first person that can put in more face to face hours than the person attending school or with a full time job, the money might be better spent on someone who can manage the staff and time, plus bring resources to the table such as the ability to find consignment uniforms, future consultants, designers, choreographers, and technicians.

Answering the question of "how much the staff should be paid," isn't an easy one, but splitting the cost into the following line items helps:

- Time
- Choreography/Design
- Band Camp
- Travel
- Technicians

Finally, when it comes to pay, recognize that everyone deserves to be paid for their time, but not everyone needs to be paid the same rate. Whoever you hire, it's important to have ongoing conversations regarding the dollars paid out versus dollars coming into the program. This conversation will help your guard staff continue to remain budget conscious.

When you do find the right person and you want them to stay with you and build the color guard over several years, ask them two crucial questions:

"How can I help you on a day to day basis?"

"How can the parents best support your efforts?"

Note: *Keep in mind that many guard instructors you hire will be inexperienced. Encourage them to* *continue to grow their skill set through additional workshops or education. Ask them to obtain a mentor to bounce ideas and problems off of.*

7 Budgeting for the Color Guard

Here is something you should know. The color guard doesn't need brand new silks, brand new costumes, and brand new equipment every season. They just don't. What you need is a guard staff that understands how to design a show around the budget. If the guard does need new costumes, then they don't have to be custom made. In fact, custom made anything is lost in the shuffle when a guard doesn't have the skills to bring that level of detailing to life. What the guard staff needs is a good understanding of the current inventory and the key elements of the show they are designing. Your new guard instructor should first inventory every silk, rifle, pole, bolt, roll of tape and any other odd thing they find in the guard room. **Make a list and then monitor that list as if it's gold sitting in Fort Knox.** The little items such as crutch tips and bolts matter and could quickly deplete the budget if not inventoried. The following is a list of items your guard staff will need to start off on a successful track.

Level One

- Flag poles that are all the same size in height and diameter
- Weights and crutch tips to make the poles spin at the exact same rate of speed and rotation
- Tape to keep the silk on the pole
- One good practice silk per performer

That's it. That is all you need to **start** the guard off on a successful track. These items will get you through the initial training process. Don't let anyone tell you differently. Now, as we all know, the guard will eventually have to buy more silks to help bring the show to life, plus costumes, and maybe even rifles and sabres. So let's discuss that.

When buying silks and costumes for the show, your guard director must first have a strong understanding of the show for which they are designing. This will require design meetings where the show is mapped out in terms of the change of mood and how you want that shift in mood brought to life. Do they need a new silk for each song or can they use pieces of fabric to dance with? Will they need props or flats to create a scene? If props are needed, keep in mind that they will have to be transported and will need parents to help build them and set them up. Every dollar counts and every time someone changes their mind, it costs money. Get it right from the beginning. Setting the budget requires significant levels of communication with the design team and the parents. You don't want to design at such a level you price kids out of your program.

Level Two

- Costumes
- Show silks
- Rifles
- Sabres
- Props, fabric, and other items to bring the show to life
- Floor tarps
- Dance shoes
- Gloves
- Knee pads
- Additional poles and the crutch tips and weights that accompany them
- Alternate size equipment such as smaller poles for swing flags or taller poles for large flags

Level two budget items may not be required items, but if you want to set the production up for visual success, then they are highly recommended. Many of these items are necessary for purposes of the show design. There is no criteria in the country that requires a color guard in marching band to have any of these items, but the production value matters. Additional items such as knee pads and gloves should be considered for safety purposes as they protect wear and tear on the body. There is also something to be said about the pride the performers have for their program. The better they feel about themselves, the more likely they will be to return. It is important to note however, that some of the best color guards work with modest budgets. In addition, if the performers cannot utilize the new equipment properly, then the new equipment is simply a waste of money. This is where overextending the budget often goes awry. Poor planning, lack of communication, and ease of online ordering can spiral the budget out of control. Just because you can order from an expensive costume company doesn't mean you should. Your guard staff should be budget conscious, even thrifty in the creation of color guard shows. This should be an expectation, and possibly a potential deal breaker in retaining their services for the following year. **It is not necessary to have brand new silks for every song to be successful.** Previously used silks can be effective if they are kept in good condition.

**Always remember to factor into the budget items that will last more than one season such as additional flag poles, weights for the poles, sabres, and practice flags. These items should last several seasons and will decrease the budget over time if factored into a multi-season budget and inventory is strictly monitored.*

When you are setting the budget for the show, map out with your staff where you want the biggest show impact to be and spend the bulk of the budget there. If you know that the costume needs to be theme based, then start there. If you need backdrops or a set to be designed that encloses the band on a smaller stage, because the band is smaller than the field you are marching on, then start there. If you know your performers will take a couple of years to get comfortable spinning, dancing, and performing, then the more visual with you can make the show with non-traditional equipment, the better.

Regardless of where you start, do everything in your power to be budget conscious and expect the guard staff to do the same. Sometimes the best shows are the ones with uncomplicated looking silks and costumes. One of the best winter guard shows of all time used one simple white flag for the entire back half of the show. It is not necessary to spend money on custom made items if the performers are not trained properly. I can't say that enough. If the performers do not demonstrate training and cannot do what they have been asked to do efficiently, then the "fancy items" won't matter. When budgeting for the show, budget for the ability of the kids you have and the booster's ability to fundraise; keep in mind that the general effect you are seeking can often be achieved with a little brainstorming and out of the box thinking. Also remember that not everything has to be bought already made. Silks can be hand sewn and designed without going through a corporate design company and some costumes can even be bought at local box stores.

Level 3

- Digitally printed flags
- Custom made costumes
- Custom created make-up designs
- Uniform additions such as hair pieces and jewels

Level three budget items simply are not necessary to make the color guard successful until they reach the upper echelon of the activity. When you pay for anything that is custom made, then you are paying for the time of the designer and costs of production. Sometimes, the fancier the equipment becomes, the more likely it is to be a distraction than support, especially if the performers don't make what is bought look good. **Money spent does not equal points gained.** Use caution and do your research before going down this path. Does the guard really need a $45 silk or can a similar style be found through online consignment stores or pre-made silks?

Custom made equipment:
Custom made costumes, silks, and floor tarps take time and extra money. Plan accordingly and take delivery times very seriously so you can get the most out of your purchase.

If it is deemed that custom made costumes and silks are important for your show to be successful, then monitor the inventory closely and think about selling those items at the end of the season, as most custom made designs aren't useful for the next season.

Level 4

- Guard jackets
- Tee shirts
- Flag bags
- Duffle bags
- Warm up outfits

Level four budget items are great items to make the guard feel unified and helps to create pride, but this will not guarantee success in score or success in recruitment. With the extra costs you may lose a few members who will not be able to afford these items. Before making these items a requirement, make sure the budget and the budget of the parents can support these unnecessary items.

Simply put, spending money is not necessary for a color guard or marching band to be successful. Yes, it looks nice, but rarely does a band program succeed by just looking nice. It takes preparation, communication, training, a solid visual design, and a well thought out cleaning process to truly bring a show to life. Most importantly, the budget for the color guard must be set with an understanding of the community in which the band exists and the ability of the boosters to fundraise without financially taxing the already taxed parents. If parents believe money is being wasted without the success they expect to come with that money, then you will be in a constant financial tug-of-war with the booster organization.

8 Running Rehearsals With The Color Guard

One of the main grievances guard staff have while working with the marching band is trying to function in conjunction with other sections during rehearsals. The guard is a unique section in that the staff is restricted in the ways they can teach the show without the performers being present at all rehearsals. The guard work cannot be written without the elements of staging and drill laid out first. So as much as the guard staff would like to write the show as early as the band receives their music, it is practically impossible to do so without the drill and counts that accompany it. This alone creates a significant level of stress for the staff as they try to fight the clock to finish the show in a reasonable amount of time in preparation for the first performance. With the stress of time looming, it is crucial that the guard staff is included in design meetings from the beginning, as well as having a direct line to the drill writer to discuss ideas and potential problems.

Training new color guard members is a long and arduous process. Young performers must learn to coordinate their bodies with the equipment and then include movement under that. Then they must take into account how to do those same skills in wind and rainy conditions. Teaching choreography and getting it on the field takes hours, and it oftentimes looks as if the color guard is falling behind the band. When the band is staging the second and third songs, the color guard could just be finishing the choreography of the first song. As a color guard grows with the same instructor, this process becomes easier as the performers become accustomed to the teaching style of that instructor or staff. As tempting as it is to rush through the process of writing equipment work and choreography, many color guard performers simply don't have the skills to move quickly. Their minds need time to adjust to what the body is asking of it. Moving with haste is ultimately a drain on much needed time later in the season as the performers will learn to adjust by cheating through work and drill, thus forcing the instructional staff to have to reteach parts of the show. For this reason, it is important that the color guard has their own sectionals or class time to learn and review the choreography.

Once the band and color guard come together as one on the field to stage and clean the show, there is a trap many band directors and program coordinators fall into regarding the color guard. Often times, more than not actually, the guard is staged along the perimeter of the band. This can create somewhat of a visual blind spot for the person responsible for running rehearsal. The trap in this is thinking that the guard staff is taking care of all of the staging and drill that is color guard related. The guard is virtually invisible to many band directors. Running rehearsal this way will not just frustrate your color guard staff, but also the performers. They will begin to sense the disconnect and not feel completely a part of the band program. It is not the band **and** guard. It is simply the band program. Acknowledging the color guard as an equal aspect of the staging and drill will not just help in the overall ensemble and effect scores, but also go a long way in building unity within the sections of the marching band. Doing this doesn't just include complimenting the guard when they deserve it, but also holding them responsible for the same rules and criticisms the winds and percussion are held to.

Color guard members who are new to the activity have a lot on their plate in terms of training, conditioning, choreography, and design. The more that drum corps and nationally based winter guards continue to push the boundaries of athleticism within the art, the more it filters down to the local levels of inexperienced youth. Keep this in mind as you watch the show come to life.

There are several rehearsal techniques that can help guard members grow in their understanding of how to move and spin at the same time. Isolating drill from equipment work helps performers focus only on the aspects of moving their feet. Then, isolating the equipment work from the drill will help them focus on their hands. It's important to switch back and forth so the muscle memory of the hands begins to merge with the muscle memory of the feet. Color guard performers often struggle with visualizing how the drill and equipment move together. The more they are on the field and in their drill sets, the more they will start to understand how choreography works with the stage. Additionally, this method works very well with the musicians as well. Drill and then hands. Hands and then drill. Then both.

Reminder: *If musical changes are made to the show, don't forget to inform the guard staff so choreography can be adjusted.*

Anyone can see a performer struggling to achieve a phrase or struggling to move their feet with the equipment work that has been given to them. It is obvious to even to most novice of audience members when the color guard does not spin or move well. The band director must feel empowered to address these issues with the color guard staff and even with the performers. Don't be afraid to encourage the color guard on the new skills they are learning, and don't be afraid to address the issues the performers seem to be facing with your color guard director. This dialog will help the band director understand the issues, allowing them to run a better rehearsal with all sections equally involved. In the end, a color guard falls under the ultimate direction of the band director for the majority of schools and he or she is responsible for the success of the entire program. Try phrasing the question of progress in this way:

"I've noticed that the performers have been struggling with the work for quite some time. Can you tell me how the cleaning process of this phrase is going? Would you like us to run it a few extra times with the band to help build consistency?"

There are significant issues spoken about on judging panels across the country regarding the color guard and its role within the band proper. Because the color guard is often over looked at practice or because the color guard staff was hired without proper vetting, many issues arise that will not just impact the color guards score and placement, but also the bands general effect, ensemble analysis, and individual analysis scores. The following are common comments related to the color guard as spoken by judges.

Poor transitions while changing equipment

"The transition from song one to song two is distracting as the written drill has a functional base to it and is not cohesive with the band

A guard cannot just run from one song to the other to exchange equipment. It is distracting and demonstrates poor planning on the part of the drill writer or guard staff. Transitions are equally important, if not more important, than the equipment being exchanged. The effect is diminished if the transition is poorly constructed and distracts from other elements of the band.

Ability of the lower body to stay in time

"The color guard is struggling to keep basic time with their feet causing a distortion in the control of the form."

The color guard must demonstrate the ability to show lower body control while marching as much as the winds and percussion. Often times the color guard struggles with moving their feet in time with the music which creates problems in maintaining form control. A solution to this is to assign a marching technician to the color guard and to hold the color guard staff accountable for not just cleaning the upper body, but the lower body as well.

Musicality

"What I'm hearing is not what I'm seeing from your color guard at this point and time."

This is a tricky one. It is important that not just the written choreography has a base of musicality, but the major effects as well. Mapping out or creating a storyboard with all major effects before the drill is written and any silks or costumes are purchased is a great way to make sure everyone is on the same page as to where all the major moments are. Plus you will save money down the road by not wasting money on unnecessary items.

Visual disconnect with the band

"I'm struggling to find the focus as the color guard has moved away from the band to the opposite side of the field."

There are many bands out there that do not write the color guard as an equal visual element within the written drill. There are several schools of thought to this, but leaving the color guard on the perimeter of the band throughout the show will begin to look repetitive. Passing the color guard through the band without paying attention to how the equipment work will fit while moving through musicians also creates poor transitions and visual eyesores. Small color guards should be carefully staged with the rest of the drill in mind and rarely should they be separated on the sides of the band. **And speaking of small guards...they too can be successful.** There is no judging criteria anywhere that states the guard needs to be above a particular number in size. Small guards can be more competitive than the bigger guards by the smart use of staging choices.

The guard and band proper should mirror each other in concept such as the use of consistent visual elements through poses and arm/hand positions. Simply put, by not including the color guard into the overall picture, will create problems with all visual captions.

Over written choreography

"The choreography throughout the production does not appear to be developmentally appropriate for the performers."

HUGE PROBLEM. Let me repeat...this is a huge problem with color guards around the country. There is nothing that states color guards must have a certain level of risk during their marching band show. In fact, most guards score better with less risk and fewer counts utilized within the phrase. There is an acceptable learning curve to achieving the written book. If the performers can't do the phrase within that curve and the staff can't get the phrase clean, then the phrase must be changed. A common trap many color guard directors fall into is the belief that they must write above the skills of the performers to prepare them for winter guard season. Many color guard instructors use marching band as the training ground for winter, but not in the way they should. It is not appropriate to write in a difficult toss or advanced dance skill when it is not developmentally appropriate. Think of it this way. Children do not learn to do multiplication before they learn the do addition, just because one day it is expected they must learn their multiplication tables. Basic fundamentals must be understood before moving on to advanced work. Each season, whether it be fall or winter, should be viewed independently of the other when it comes to the written book.

Ego is often a driver of over written choreography. Some instructors want to impress their friends. Others use a less experienced guard to gain enough notoriety to move on to more prestigious jobs. This cannot be allowed. Choreography must be written to the skill level of the performers, the concept, and the season for which it is being written.

Poor training to manage the written book or movement choreography

"The color guard does not demonstrate an understanding of body mechanics to successfully achieve the phrase."

This phrase spoken by a judge will impact just about every visual caption on the judge's sheets. Training must be demonstrated in both equipment and body. If the training does not exist, it will be shown by frequent drops, inability to recover from mistakes, poor marching skills while manipulating equipment and inability to blend with the performers around them. It isn't rocket science to spot a poorly trained guard and good judges know the difference between a bad show day versus a bad show.

No one can hide the lack of training. It will mostly surely come out in how the performer holds their posture throughout the phrase, which shows a basic understanding of muscular dynamics.

As a band director, it is perfectly acceptable to address any one of these issues with the color guard staff. Color guard is not the special exception to the band and neither is the guard staff. Yes, the guard staff brings special skills to the program, but it doesn't exempt them from answering for the progress of the performers. The best way to counter any one of the previous judges' comments is to build the communication with your guard staff as open and free. Everyone is on the same team and should be on the same page. Unfortunately, there are too many times where the band director writes off the color guard as "other duties as assigned" or the guard staff writes off the marching band season to just get to winter guard season. Both are damaging to the show, the kids, and the program.

9 To Have or not to Have A Winter Guard

Making the decision to have a winter guard should not be made lightly or in isolation by the color guard staff. Winter guard is usually the favorite season of most guard instructors because of the autonomy of design, ability to move at their own pace, and additional time to train performers. Having a winter guard can be great for recruitment through the ongoing building of the guards' identity and has the ability to create a more cohesive group that works at a faster pace with the marching band.

The benefits to having a winter guard are endless. Winter guard has become the place for guard people to feel special. For your staff, this is their opportunity to showcase their skills as designers, choreographers, and technicians while receiving direct feedback from judges for their work in the captions of design and training. For young or inexperienced instructors, winter guard is usually a "wake up call" that highlights their strengths and weaknesses by a system of criteria that directly spells out class based expectations. It is also a safe bet that if you choose to have a winter guard, the performers will become more invested with the marching band program and more apt to stay throughout their tenure of high school. Winter guard keeps your performers engaged year-round and, to be honest, it often times keeps your staff engaged as well.

Winter guard, however, is not an easy endeavor and even guards who don't have strong competitive goals will need significant levels of planning. Just as in marching band, if the guard staff doesn't have clearly spelled out goals and processes, then the time and money spent will just lead to waste. Winter guard takes on many forms. For the most part, there are three types of competitive classes:

- National
- Local/Regional
- Exhibition/Rating.

Deciding in which type of class your color guard should participate should be guided by the strategic goals that coincide with the larger goals of the music program as a whole. The category descriptions are as follows:

National

Nationally based guards are color guards that perform at, or have aspirations to perform at, the Winter Guard International (WGI) World Championships which are currently being held in Dayton, Ohio. National guards may go every year or every couple of years, but the overall goal is to compete on the national stage.

These color guard programs should be very experienced and have a strong base of fundraising. Their rehearsals are more intense, more time consuming, and they attend at least one sanctioned regional if not two or three each season. They tend to travel more and their budgets often include a multitude of staff members, as well as consultants. Guards who compete on the national stage are held to extremely high standards based on very specific criteria and the competition itself is aggressive and intense. The judges are seasoned and well-trained. Nationally based guards need a strong base of training and design, and the performers need to be mentally resilient and have a robust physical stamina.

Local/Regional

This is the largest base of winter guards in the country. There are literally thousands of winter guards around the United States and Europe that never compete at the WGI level in terms of national aspirations. Local and Regional color guards belong to their local circuit and through that local circuit compete in one of a number of classes. Each local circuit structures their base of classes differently, but most function under the WGI class model of Regional A, A, Open, and World Class. Classes defined as A and Regional A are usually broken down further based on skill level of the performers and design ability of the staff. These guards may or may not rehearse as much as a nationally based guard and, sometimes these guards are just as good as color guards who attend nationals, but for reasons that are as individual as the units themselves, have chosen to stay local. Sometimes these guards will attend a WGI Regional, but their primary goal is to remain local.

Exhibition/Rating

These color guards are local based guards that either don't have the resources to fully compete or the program is not set up in such a way to allow for a competitive program. These color guards rehearse a few times in the winter and the goal is usually to provide a performance opportunity to the kids and give them a taste of winter guard. These guards usually attend one or two local circuit shows without fully joining the circuit or attend a festival style show for feedback and rating only.

Answering the question as to whether you should or should not have a winter guard is complex and should actually be made well before the competitive marching band season has even begun. Winter guard takes careful planning and rarely does a winter guard survive if, within the planning process, the business of the program is overshadowed by the design of the show.

The questions you should ask of your staff and the questions they should be asking themselves are:

Where will the guard practice?

When will the guard practice?

What is the budget by line item?

How much will winter guard cost the performers?

Where will you perform?

Will you be hiring or bringing in additional staff members?

How will you transport the guard to competitions?

How will winter guard better the marching band?

What is the expectation you have of me as the band director?

Oftentimes a young or inexperienced color guard staff will think that having a winter guard is the natural continuation or sometimes the evolution of the marching band. However, the staff may not think through the logistics of running a winter ensemble without the support and resources of the overall band program. Many booster organizations will not fund a winter guard due to misinformation on how the winter guard fits into the overall picture of the music program. Other problems may include a lack of administrative support regarding facilities. Many winter guards find it difficult locating a consistent rehearsal space that protects the performers from the winter elements, fits a standard gym size floor tarp, and allows the performers enough height to toss equipment.

As much as a winter guard can help build a color

guard program, it can also hurt the program if mismanaged. If the decision is made to form a winter guard, the kids will be committed to color guard for the entire year and that commitment can be taxing; there are virtually no breaks between seasons. Once winter is over, many programs start again with the preparation for marching band. It can burn out the kids, the staff, and the boosters who have to fundraise for all ensembles. If you have an inexperienced staff, then their lack of long term-logistical planning can create havoc while they try to navigate the reservation of rehearsal space, management of money, and travel. It is important that as a band director, you don't abandon the color guard once winter season starts. The performers in the winter guard need moral support, but also advocacy that comes from the person that sits at the top of program. If you don't have the time or desire to do this, then make sure you are honest with the staff going into it.

Directing a winter guard is the perceived crowning jewel of most color guard instructors at some point in their guard careers. They dream of standing among the elite of the activity and envision their program among the best at WGI. Most though, never make it to that moment. There are many more guards that never make it to WGI than do.

The business of managing a winter guard makes it difficult to focus on the design of the show, and many instructors simply don't have the administrative and time management skills to truly develop the guard for the national level. Many will struggle with the art of influence that allows them to barter for rehearsal space. Financing floor tarps and costumes get in the way of designing them. Managing performers and parents on a daily basis can ruin a perfectly planned out rehearsal schedule. In the process of managing a guard, many guard staff will seek to move on to an easier program. They want to find the place where the grass is greener, but as we all know, the grass is never greener...and the weeds still have to be pulled and the land still has to be cultivated. Thus, bringing us back to to the person youthe person you are hiring and thethe skills you need them to have.. The right director may not be able to design the best show, but will certainly be able to communicate their needs so others will want to contribute resources to make it successful. That success includes administration, parents, community partners, other instructors, designers and you...the band director.

Winter guard is an amazing arena of performance for guard members who don't have the winter privilege of musical training that concert season brings your musicians. Most guard programs in the country are in close enough proximity to a local circuit that offers several performance opportunities. Those circuits are governed by a board of directors and the shows are usually run very well. It is in your best interest as a band director to get in touch with your local circuit and learn their show guidelines, membership fees, and the administrative board of directors responsible for the day to day operations. Circuit administrators can walk you through any questions and may have resources available that you are unaware of.

Heed this warning:
Not all programs can handle a winter guard and most programs cannot start and should not start by declaring that they will be a national based program until there is a solid foundation of training, flow of money, and rehearsal space.

10 WHEN TO RE-EVALUATE YOUR STAFF

There comes a time in almost every program when the band director must make a decision whether to retain the services of the current guard director or the entire staff or move to search for others. There are several reasons for this and they, like all other decisions, are as individual as the kids that you teach. The need to retain staff doesn't necessarily mean the staff member(s) has become a problem. It might simply be that the current color guard staff has outgrown the success of the program, needing a more talented or modern group of designers and technicians. Another reason could be that the resources of the program can't keep up with the salaries and expectations of the staff. The reasons listed above should follow the strategic direction of your overall intended goals.

Changing guard staffs happen frequently and many programs will turn their guard staff over every year. This is a problem and does nothing to build consistency. This should be an indicator of a larger problem that is occurring with the band director and/or boosters that must be addressed before the program will be able to see any type of real success. A band director has the duty to evaluate their full staff at the end of each season or school year for a number of reasons that can include:

- Staff cohesiveness
- Ability to manage students
- Parental complaints/compliments
- Management of money
- Philosophical difference in teaching styles
- Lack of competitive success
- Lack of talent

During the school year, it is important to have regularly scheduled staff meetings and updates with your guard staff so the person responsible for all ensembles of the band can better understand the needs of the guard, but also counter any problems that may be on the horizon. It's important to recognize when the guard staff is in over their heads in terms of management, design, or training. Regular meetings will help identify problems such as knowing how much money is outgoing versus incoming. Asking direct and open ended questions about how the performers are handling the schedule will help counter potential parental complaints and issues with school and homework. You should ask to see recaps and randomly listen to audio files of judge commentary from shows and competitions. Sit in on critiques at winter guard competitions if possible. This approach is not a violation of the trust of the staff, but should be seen as you being a well-informed band director. The band director has to answer to the boosters and school administration. They are asked to advocate for resources of the guard and only by being well informed will that advocacy be effective.

If you find that your staff is on constant defense, then you should think about re-evaluating who is on your staff. A guard staff should feel comfortable taking feedback from judges and other staff members. A staff that trusts each other share their concerns with each other. Should the guard staff tell you, the band director, that the band is not playing well during a particular part? Should the percussion caption head get involved in the choreographic phrasing of the guard? Probably not, because they are not hired to teach outside their captions, but the band director must feel empowered to address all the sections...including the color guard. For example, let's say that you have noticed that it is the middle of the season and the guard has dropped the same toss consistently in every run through. This is worthy of a conversation about simplifying the book. It is perfectly acceptable for a band director to say that it appears that the guard is struggling on a specific part and maybe it would help to review a section several times with the band and percussion, because everyone could stand to put in a little more work on that part. It is when your director or instructor fights every comment with an excuse, thus showing they are incapable of taking feedback and evaluating their program, that red flags should be raised.

There are many band directors out there who simply

don't want to deal with the color guard. They want the guard to be as invisible as possible, but also successful. On the other side of the coin there are guard instructors that want the band director and boosters nowhere near the color guard, but want their resources and support when it's time for checks to be written. Neither can have it that way. It won't work, and neither party will get what they want. If you are finding that you don't want to deal with the color guard staff or the color guard staff doesn't want to deal with you, then it's time to look at how the guard is being managed.

11 UNETHICAL STAFF MEMBERS

As difficult as it may be to have to fire a staff member who is a good person, but no longer the right fit for the program, there is a much more stressful decision to make that is less about programmatic decisions and more about behavior. Unfortunately, the world of color guard is not immune from unethical behaviors that plague youth based activities and many band directors have found themselves on the receiving end of scandals that involve youth, because of such behaviors. The worst thing that could happen in your band program, and to the kids with whom you are entrusted, is the allegation of sexual abuse. Color guard and marching band is not immune and a simple Google search will list a number of color guard instructors who have been fired and charged with sexual battery of a minor. In many of those cases, other staff members knew, including the band director. Forming a relationship with performers must always remain in the form of mentor and coach and the very second you see those lines crossed, as difficult as it is, you must act by informing the authorities governed by your requirements of being a teacher and school employee. The signs you should be looking for are as follows:

- Contact with students outside of the written policy of communication for the overall music program
- Texting individual students
- Friending individual students on a personal Facebook or social media account
- Talking about an individual student more than others and in a way that appears to be obsessive or inappropriate
- Grooming students by buying them personal items
- Invitations by the instructor for a minor to participate in outside events that do not include pageantry related activities
- Taking photos of the performers that are not rehearsal or performance related
- Refusing to let parents attend practice, thus isolating the guard staff from watchful eyes
- Finding a staff member alone in a room or a private space with a student

It is in your best interest to follow your gut on these issues, professional protocol and **when in doubt check it out.** You are not just saving your job and possibly your freedom, but the goal should always be to protect the kids from harm.

There are other problems that present themselves that may require an investigation into accusations. The mishandling of funds is a topic that comes up often in color guard circles because of the easy and consistent access to money. Guard instructors buy and order supplies for the guard. Misunderstandings can easily be taken care of upon hiring staff if guidelines are set outlining the exact procedures that money will be handled and supplies will be bought. The procedures should detail who handles financial items such as:

- Money collected for dues
- Purchase orders, vendor contracts
- Staff negotiation and pay
- Small local purchases such as building supplies for props
- Management of fundraisers

Once these policies are spelled out with a sign off form, it will be easier to spot mistakes in money management vs. the deliberate mishandling of funds. Skimming off the top of fundraisers and student dues can be a problem that raises its ugly head every once in a while if there is not official oversight of the money by a secondary organization such as the booster club or school treasurer. Another problem related to money is a guard instructor or contractor using friends as vendors without checking for comparable rates on items such as the design of costumes, silks, and other supplies.

Probably though, the paramount issue related to the mismanagement of funds is simply the lack of the guard staff to show budgetary concern. Spending without conscience is not illegal, but it's

> extremely irresponsible. There is a manipulative game often played in the pageantry world, where those who instruct and design will often influence or exploit those who write the checks into believing that spending excessive amounts of money is necessary for success. That is simply not true.

A serious problem arises with band directors who have issues with a staff member whose teaching sytle counters the philosophy of the band as a whole and when that teaching style becomes abusive and harmful. There was a time in our activity when yelling and screaming seemed like the most effective method of teaching. It was common practice for voices to be raised in fits of anger over counts not being achieved or equipment drops during a show. There are stories of guard equipment, drum sticks, gock blocks, and even shoes being thrown at guard members. Other stories include exercise for punishment that bordered on abuse and water being withheld on a hot sunny day until a certain goal was achieved. Those days are gone. Even the United States military has learned better ways of training recruits that don't include abusive actions. Common sense should be exercised when identifying whether or not a staff member is being abusive or just demanding. Listen to the kids when they report abuse with an open mind. All reports should be taken seriously, but it is important to discern whether or not the staff member in question is being abusive or exercising a strict teaching style. Clearly, a fireable offense should fall into the same category that professional teachers must adhere to. Name calling, foul language, excessive use of exercise for punishment, deliberately withholding safety precautions such as water or knee pads, bullying, and the sanctioning of hazing are examples of fireable offenses.

Working with young people is not a game. Too many stories from too many bands have surfaced in the past two decades of staff members getting fired, arrested, sent to prison, and serving life on the sexual predator registry. Band directors and booster organizations have been taken down with the name of the criminal. As in life, most people are very good and well-meaning individuals, but there are some that don't have the best interest of youth at heart and you **must** take action if you find those people in front of your performers.

Warning: ***Your staff may be friendly with the performers of the program, but they may not be friends with them.***

12 CONCLUSION

We have this one chance with the kids we teach. We owe it to those who trust us with their time and money to create the best program possible, with a staff that works well together, communicates honestly, and seeks to consistently better themselves. As I sit here writing this final chapter, and having been involved with the pageantry activity for over 30 years as a performer, director, technician, designer, board member, and judge; I realize that I have enough perspective on the marching arts to look at young instructors today and realize that they have inherited an activity that has developed as an art form and sport, and has come to age in a world that is very different than the one I grew up in.

Today, instructors must be versed in not just nuances of design, but also in concepts related to dance and theater. They must have an awareness of the physical conditioning required to achieve an ever demanding equipment and movement vocabulary. Many are experienced in software applications for the editing of music and creation of storyboards.

Additionally, through the damaging effects of a molestation scandal at Penn State and the death of the drum major by institutional hazing at FAMU, all youth activities have now changed. What is expected today in terms of professionalism and knowledge is not what was expected twenty years ago. Risk management, ethics, safety, budgeting, and coaching with absolute intent is an expectation of the job. In today's world, many instructors are hired by the school district as adjunct teachers and receive benefits such as health care and retirement accounts. Most all districts require background checks and some are beginning to require additional training such as risk management and ethics. Professional expectations are higher than they ever were before and for a good reason. Hire your staff with care and diligence and set the precedent that ongoing education for all staff...including yourself...will be a priority of the program.

Through the technology of drill writing software, computerized design applications, and even social media; instructors today can become entrepreneurs of the pageantry arts and form their own design and consulting companies due to the quick transfer of information, goods, and services. There has never been a better opportunity for someone to make a career out of color guard and that is a GREAT thing for our activity. However, be on the lookout for instructional staff and companies that over extend themselves and don't show your band the attention it deserves. I can't stress it enough. Require references, ask questions, and get contracts in place.

The people who stay in the color guard activity as instructors and designers are passionate to the point of obsession. Many of them treat their art no different than the art you see hanging in a gallery or presented on the theatrical stage. They are some of the hardest working and most creative people around as they work late into the night designing the perfect costume for your guard. They have to combine art with sport and figure out how to stay current in a world that changes virtually every season. The creativity that pours out of these people is undervalued and underfunded as a public art form, but keeping that creativity flowing with extremely long hours and minimal amounts of money is an amazing fete to witness. At the heart of color guard is passion and within that passion is a creative drive that sits at the core of those that coach the performers, design the shows, and clean the choreography. In the course of managing a band program please do not forget that there is a color guard instructor out there needing your support.

My hope is that if you take one thing away from this book, it will be that support through ongoing communication, your physical presence in acknowledging the guard, and advocacy with administration will ultimately build your guard as you grow season by season <u>with</u> your staff.

Quick and Final Reminders

Design

Include the guard staff in design meetings and discussions and communicate their needs with the drill writer.

Rifles and sabres are not a necessity. Weapons are not a requirement for a color guard to score well. In fact, if your color guard isn't trained well, then rifles and sabres could hurt the overall score.

It isn't necessary to buy brand new every season. Equipment, costumes, silks, and floor tarps can all be reused or bought used.

Communication

No one staff member should have the sole ear of the band director. All caption heads need an equal voice if you want to build a staff that trusts each other.

Don't allow staff members to gossip about each other. Not all staff you hire will be mature and professional. Set the precedent early on.

The Kids

Don't forget that guard members aren't always musicians and may struggle with complex musical phrases. Take time to help them understand the music they are performing.

Encourage a healthy lifestyle of exercise and diet so the performers are physically capable of managing the show they are asked to perform.

Patience

Be patient when building the guard program. Each season should build upon the other.

Parents

Most of the parents won't know what color guard is and depth of work it actually entails. Offer as much information up front regarding financial obligations, communication procedures, and rehearsal schedules that you can.

Parents don't always understand that color guard requires physical and mental endurance. Invite them to open rehearsals and encourage them to watch, so that they can better understand the process.

Available Podcasts

The following podcasts are available at MarchingRoundtable.com:

Episode 47: Starting a New Winter Guard

Episode 58: Training and Conditioning to Prevent Injury on the Field

Episode 119: Strategies for Combating Hazing and Bullying

Episode 129: Cleaning Guard Work

Episode 156: Hazing and Values

Episode 164: Advice for Young Instructors

Episode 192: Creating Effect with a Non-Traditional Color Guard

Episode 244: Inappropriate Show Concepts

Episode 452: Class A Color Guard - Building a Legacy

Episode 453: Class A Color Guard - How to Succeed in Dayton

Episodes 468/469/470: Winter Guard Music Choices

Episode 486: Is the Color Guard Tail Wagging the Marching Band Dog?

Episode 487: Solutions for Balancing the Importance of Color Guard in Marching Band

Episode 488: Are We Overvaluing the Color Guard in Marching Band?

Episode 489: Are We Overvaluing the Color Guard in Marching Band? Pt. 2

Episode 490: Balancing Color Guard in Marching Band Through Coordination

Episode534: Women's Issues in the Marching Arts

Episode 535: Women's Issues, Pt. 2 –Solutions

Episode 557: Ethics and Risk Management for Instructors

Episode 558: Protect Yourself from Litigation – Risk Management for Instructors

Additional Information and Resources

For more information please refer to the following resources:

General Information

Winter Guard International

http://www.wgi.org/contents/This-is-WGI.html

Winter Guard International Circuit Partners

http://www.wgi.org/circuits.php

Marching Roundtable Academy

www.marchingroundtableacademy.com

Marching Roundtable Judges Academy

https://judgesacademy.com/

Equipment and Costume Companies

Algy

http://www.algyteam.com/

A Wish Come True

http://www.awctcolorguard.com/

The Band Hall

https://thebandhall.com/

Field and Floor Fx

http://www.fieldandfloorfx.com/

Fred J. Miller, Inc.

https://www.fjminc.com/

McCormick's

http://www.mccormicksnet.com/products/home/

Facebook Pages

Women of Color Guard

https://www.facebook.com/womenofcolorguard/

Color Guard Questions and Answers

https://www.facebook.com/groups/CGFAQ/?fref=nf

Post Script

When I joined the winter guard in 1987 at McGavock High School, I had no idea what path it would take me down and what journey I would find myself on. I just simply did it because a friend of mine said it might be a "cool thing" to try. Thirty years later, and I'm still trying to make sense out of this ever evolving activity of ours. At times, I feel as if I still don't have a grasp of where we are headed and with each new person I meet, I realize how far we have come and how far we have to go. This art we toil over called color guard wraps us in a blanket of emotion day in and day out and that emotion is the universal power that lets us know we are still alive. We spend hours laboring over drill on the hot summer fields of band camp and wrap ourselves up in knots trying to make sense of the new choreography presented in Dayton, Ohio each April.

I decided to write this book after three years of writing my blog "Growing Up Pageantry." Over the years I received numerous comments and questions about how we can better work with the music side of the marching arts. Email after email came to me with questions about best practices in working with the band director during marching band season. I found that I didn't have any more of an answer than I did when I started my first teaching job back in 1993. So, I set out to ask questions of my peers and analyze my own experiences. I looked at the progression from the hiring process, through band camp, competition season, and the forming of the winter guard. In my conversations I found that what most instructors wanted was support. So that's where this book comes from. It's a look at how we can best support each other and form the instructional team the kids are entitled to.

The near future will bring about several books as I take a look at how we can better help performers grow to be amazing and professional instructors, the role of women in the pageantry arts, and the journey we take as we grow from a little activity to a professional industry.

ABOUT THE AUTHOR

Shelba Waldron has a history in the marching arts that spans thirty years from performer to instructor and board member to judge. She spent her performing years learning from the best in the activity at McGavock High School in Nashville, Tn. and then continuing on to the Star of Indiana Drum and Bugle Corps and Pride of Cincinnati Winter Guard. After aging out, Shelba went on to instruct throughout Florida at several world class programs for the next two decades such as Shaktai Performance Company, Alliance of Miami, and Paradigm Winter Guards. She has spent the past twelve years at Paradigm as the Technical Director and is proud to continue to consult with Paradigm after helping turn the staff over to previous members she taught. Shelba has judged for WGI and throughout the nation in both the fall and winter seasons.

In her professional life, she has a Master's Degree in Criminal Justice and is a sought out expert in the field of youth development. She speaks nationally on the topics of youth development trends, bullying, substance abuse, and risk management when working with youth. After 23 years of working in the field of youth development, she has chosen to start her own consulting firm called Forward Youth Consulting, where she consults on the management and sustainability of youth programs and coaching minors with deliberate intent.

Shelba has a nine year old son named Joshua who keeps her busy with his activities and is her drive to make the world a better place for children.

Made in the USA
Coppell, TX
18 May 2022

77903191R00066